Daniel
in the lions' den

Story by Penny Frank
Illustrated by Tony Morris

THE LION
STORY BIBLE

27

TRING · BATAVIA · SYDNEY

The Bible tells us how God chose the nation of Israel to be his special people. He made them a promise that he would always love and care for them. But they must obey him.

Because God's people turned away from him, they were defeated in battle and taken into exile. One of the prisoners was a man called Daniel. He was determined to be loyal to God, whatever happened.

You can find this story in the part of the Bible which has his name.

Copyright © 1987 Lion Publishing

Published by
Lion Publishing plc
Icknield Way, Tring, Herts, England
ISBN 0 85648 752 X
Lion Publishing Corporation
1705 Hubbard Avenue, Batavia,
Illinois 60510, USA
ISBN 0 85648 752 X
Albatross Books Pty Ltd
PO Box 320, Sutherland, NSW 2232, Australia
ISBN 0 86760 536 7

First edition 1987

All rights reserved

Printed and bound in Belgium

**British Library Cataloguing in
Publication Data**

Frank, Penny
Daniel in the lions' den.—(The Lion
Story Bible; 27)
1. Daniel—Juvenile literature
I. Title   II. Morris, Tony
224'.50924   BS580.D2
ISBN 0-85648-752-X

**Library of Congress Cataloging in
Publication Data**

Frank, Penny.
Daniel in the lions' den.
(The Lion Story Bible; 27)
1. Daniel, the Prophet—Juvenile
literature. 2. Bible. O.T.—Biography—
Juvenile literature. 3. Bible stories,
English—O.T. Daniel. [1. Daniel, the
Prophet. 2. Bible stories—O.T.]
I. Morris, Tony, ill. II. Title. III. Series:
Frank, Penny. Lion Story Bible; 27.
BS580.D2F73 1987   224'.509505
86-2862
ISBN 0-85648-752-X

Daniel lived in Babylon. He was not in
his own country. Daniel was a prisoner.
But because he was clever he was
chosen for work in the king's palace.

Daniel longed to be back home in
Jerusalem. He prayed to God three
times a day in his little room.

One day Babylon was captured by the
Persians. There was a new king, called
Darius. He knew that Daniel was a very
wise man, even though he was a foreign
prisoner.

Whenever he needed help and advice
the king sent for Daniel. Daniel always
asked God for the right answers.

There were many other wise men in Babylon. They were jealous of Daniel.

'Why doesn't the king call for us when he needs help,' they said, 'instead of that foreigner, Daniel?'

The wise men held a secret meeting.
    'Something will have to be done about Daniel,' they said. 'How can we get rid of him?'

'The trouble is,' one of them grumbled,
'he's such a good man. We can't get him
into trouble for anything, unless it's to
do with his God.'

The next day they went to speak to the king.

'King Darius, live for ever,' they said. 'You are the best king Babylon has ever had. Nothing is too difficult for you to do.'

The king felt most important as he listened to them.

'Why don't you make a law,' the men
went on, 'to say that for the next thirty
days the people must ask no one but
you for whatever they need. Then they'll
know how great you are.'

'What a good idea!' said the king.

Daniel was in the palace when the new law was read out. It said that anyone who disobeyed the law and asked his god for anything would be thrown into the pit where the lions were kept.

The men followed Daniel home. Then they hid where they could watch him.

'Let's hope he asks his God for something,' they whispered. 'Then we'll be rid of him.'

Daniel thought about the new law as he went home.

He always thanked God for his help and for taking care of him.

But there were things he asked for, too.

The king's law had said he must not do
that.

Daniel went to the open window. He
started to pray out loud to God, just as
he always had.

The men who were hiding nearby saw
Daniel at the window. They heard him
asking his God for what he needed.

They were so pleased. They ran to tell
the king that Daniel had broken his law.

The king was very sad. He did not want to hurt Daniel.

'I wish I hadn't made that new law,' said the king. 'Those men are only jealous. Now I shall have to throw Daniel to the lions.'

King Darius could not break his own law. He had written his own name on the paper when the law was made. The law could not be changed.

So the soldiers from the palace went to get Daniel.

They took him to the place where the lions were kept and threw him in.

The king went back to his palace. He knew how silly he had been to make a law like that.

He could not sleep.

'I do hope Daniel's God is as powerful as Daniel says he is,' the king thought. 'Perhaps he will save Daniel from the lions.'

Early the next morning, before the
palace servants were awake, King Darius
got up. Everywhere was silent. He
hurried to the lion-pit.

'Daniel, can you hear me?' the king called out. 'Has your God been able to save you from the sharp teeth of the lions?' He did not expect an answer.

'Yes, he has,' shouted back Daniel. 'They haven't opened their mouths all night. God knew I had done no wrong. I am perfectly all right.'

Quickly the king ordered his servants to pull Daniel up out of the lion-pit.

He punished the men who had been so jealous. He wrote to all the people in his great empire.

'I command you to respect Daniel's God. He is a living God and he will rule for ever. He saved Daniel from the lions.'

The Lion Story Bible is made up of 52 individual stories for young readers, building up an understanding of the Bible as one story — God's story — a story for all time and all people.

The Old Testament section (numbers 1–30) tells the story of a great nation — God's chosen people, the Israelites — and God's love and care for them through good times and bad. The stories are about people who knew and trusted God. From this nation came one special person, Jesus Christ, sent by God to save all people everywhere.

The story of *Daniel in the lions' den* comes from the Old Testament book of Daniel, chapter 6. Daniel had done nothing wrong. He was the victim of his jealous enemies.

When he was thrown into the lions' den he must have expected to be eaten alive. But instead God chose to save him, so that the king of Babylon and all his people would know that Daniel's God was the real God.

God does not always choose to save innocent people. We cannot always understand his purposes, though we know that they are good and just. God showed how much he loves us by sending his own Son, who had done nothing wrong, to give his life to save us.

The next story in this series, number 28: *Queen Esther saves her people*, tells how a pretty Jewish girl was able to foil a plot to kill the whole nation.